WHO IS
CAPTAIN
MARVEL?

Written by Nicole Reynolds

Editor Nicole Reynolds
Project Art Editor Stefan Georgiou
Senior Production Editor Siu Yin Chan
Senior Production Controller Mary Slater
Managing Editor Emma Grange
Managing Art Editor Vicky Short
Publishing Director Mark Searle

First American Edition, 2022
Published in the United States by DK Publishing
1745 Broadway, 20th Floor, New York NY 10019

DK, a Division of Penguin Random House LLC
22 23 24 25 10 9 8 7 6 5 4 3 2 1
001–329190–Oct /2022

©2022 MARVEL

A catalog record for this book is available from the Library of Congress.

ISBN 978-0-7440-6099-7 (Paperback)

ISBN 978-0-7440-6100-0 (Hardcover)

DK books are available at special discounts when purchased in bulk for sales promotions,
premiums, fund-raising, or educational use. For details, contact: DK Publishing Special Markets,
1745 Broadway, 20th Floor, New York NY10019
SpecialSales@dk.com

Printed and bound in China

For the curious

www.dk.com

This book is made from
Forest Stewardship Council™
certified paper—one small
step in DK's commitment
to a sustainable future.

Contents

Meet Captain Marvel

Carol Danvers is a powerful Super Hero. She has superhuman strength and can fire energy blasts from her hands. Carol doesn't need a spaceship to explore space. She can fly at incredible speeds and survive in outer space without a helmet!

Dreams of flight

When Carol was a child, she dreamed of exploring space. She wanted to become an astronaut. Carol worked very hard to achieve her dreams. After she finished school, Carol worked for the United States Air Force and NASA. She was one of the Air Force's best pilots!

The Kree

The Kree are tough aliens from the planet Hala. They usually have blue skin and are very strong. The Kree want to rule the universe. They have fought many wars to grow their empire.

Captain Mar-Vell

Captain Mar-Vell is a Kree
soldier. He was sent to Earth to
spy on humans. While spying
on Earth's space program he
met Carol. They became great
friends. Captain Mar-Vell grew
to like humans and protect
them from alien invaders.

Becoming Captain Marvel

One day, Carol was caught in the blast of an exploding alien device with Captain Mar-Vell. The power of the blast combined their DNA. Carol now has Kree abilities and super powers. She chose the Super Hero name Captain Marvel after Captain Mar-Vell.

Super Hero suit

Captain Marvel wears a special suit for exploring space. The blue and red colors are inspired by Captain Mar-Vell's suit. Carol is super strong. She doesn't need a very protective suit!

Hair pokes
out of helmet

Glowing hands

Sturdy boots

Shining example

Captain Marvel is a great role model and leader. Lots of other Super Heroes look up to her.

Teamwork
Carol can be stubborn but she loves to work in a team.

Mentorship
Carol inspires other Super Heroes to be their best.

Selfless
Carol always puts the welfare of others first.

Determined
Captain Marvel works hard to protect the Earth.

Adventurous
Carol loves to explore space and visit new planets.

Ms. Marvel

Kamala Khan is named Ms. Marvel. She chose her Super Hero name because she is a huge fan of Captain Marvel. Kamala fights crime in Jersey City. She can stretch her body into any shape or size.

Monica Rambeau

Monica Rambeau is a
great leader and Super Hero.
She can move at superhuman
speed and make herself
invisible. Monica uses her
amazing abilities to fight evil.
She uses the Super Hero
name Spectrum, but she
has also been known as
Captain Marvel!

Nick Fury

Nick Fury is the leader of
S.H.I.E.L.D. This group
protects the Earth from
danger. Nick works with
lots of Super Heroes, like
the Avengers. Carol has
known Nick for a long time.
They work together to keep
the planet safe.

The Avengers

The Avengers are an awesome team of Super Heroes. Carol joins the team to help them fight Super Villains and criminals. Over the years, different heroes have joined the Avengers. Carol is always proud to fight alongside them.

Guardians of the Galaxy

The Guardians of the Galaxy are a team of space adventurers and heroes. Carol teams up with them to explore more of the universe.

Peter Quill is **Star-Lord**. He is the brave leader of the team.

Gamora is one of the fiercest fighters in the galaxy.

Groot is an alien who looks like a tall walking tree.

Rocket Racoon has plenty of weapons and attitude!

Drax preferred to fight alone until he joined the team.

Tough Titan

The dangerous Super Villain Thanos will do anything to rule the galaxy. He is very strong and powerful. Thanos has access to technology that can destroy humanity. Captain Marvel must work with other Super Heroes to defeat him!

The Skrulls

The Skrulls are aliens with an unusual skill. They can shapeshift and change their appearance to look like any person or animal. They once planned to invade Earth by pretending to be Super Heroes! The Skrulls have been at war with the Kree for a long time.

Moonstone

Doctor Karla Sofen is the Super Villain Moonstone. She and Captain Marvel have fought many times. Her ability to fly and shoot laser beams comes from a moonstone. It is a special Kree gem.

Deathbird

Deathbird is a member of the Shi'ar Royal Family. The Shi'ar are aliens with birdlike features. Deathbird has large wings and super-sharp talons! She is an expert at martial arts. Deathbird fought Captain Marvel when they met on Earth.

Binary

Carol temporarily gained new powers after meeting alien scientists. For a short time, Carol changed her Super Hero name to Binary. Binary has the power of a star! She uses the energy from a white hole to fly higher and faster than ever.

The Daily Bugle

Carol is an awesome Super Hero and a great writer. She has worked as a journalist for the Daily Bugle. The Editor-in-Chief of the Daily Bugle is grumpy J. Jonah Jameson. He is very difficult to work with!

Furry friend

Carol has a pet cat named Chewie.
She may look like a cuddly kitty
but Chewie is actually an alien.

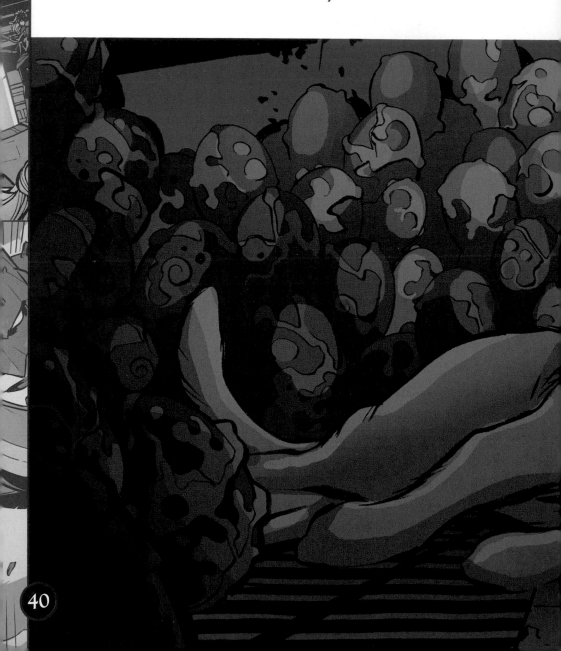

She is a dangerous species named a Flerken. They can lay eggs that hatch into kittens!

Cosmic protector

Captain Marvel is determined to protect the people of Earth. She is always ready to fight for justice. Carol can fly to the rescue from anywhere in the universe!

Quiz

1. Who is the leader of the Guardians of the Galaxy?

2. What kind of alien is Chewie?

3. Which planet do the Kree come from?

4. Where does Kamala Khan live?

5. What was young Carol's dream job?

6. Which Super Hero goes by the name Spectrum?

7. Who did Carol work with
at the Daily Bugle?

8. True or false? Deathbird is a member
of the Shi'ar Royal Family.

9. What is the Skrull's unusual power?

10. Who was sent to Earth
to spy on humans?

Glossary

determined
wanting to do
something very much,
even if it is difficult

empire
a group of nations
ruled by one person,
government, or nation

invader
an army or nation
that uses force to
enter and take over
another nation

journalist
a person who writes
stories for a newspaper,
magazine, radio,
or television

martial arts
a traditional type of
fighting or defending
yourself

mentorship
giving advice to
a younger or less
experienced person

welfare
the health and
happiness of a
person or animal

white hole
the reverse of a black
hole—a cosmic object
which can emit energy
and light

Index

Answers to the quiz on pages 44 and 45
1. Peter Quill (Star-Lord) 2. A Flerken 3. Hala 4. Jersey City
5. An astronaut 6. Monica Rambeau 7. J.Jonah Jameson 8. True
9. They can shapeshift 10. Captain Mar-Vell

A LEVEL FOR EVERY READER

This book is a part of an exciting four-level reading series to support children in developing the habit of reading widely for both pleasure and information. Each book is designed to develop a child's reading skills, fluency, grammar awareness, and comprehension in order to build confidence and enjoyment when reading.

Ready for a Level 2 (Beginning to Read) book

A child should:

- be able to recognize a bank of common words quickly and be able to blend sounds together to make some words.
- be familiar with using beginner letter sounds and context clues to figure out unfamiliar words.
- sometimes correct his/her reading if it doesn't look right or make sense.
- be aware of the need for a slight pause at commas and a longer one at periods.

A valuable and shared reading experience

For many children, reading requires much effort, but adult participation can make reading both fun and easier. Here are a few tips on how to use this book with a young reader:

Check out the contents together:

- read about the book on the back cover and talk about the contents page to help heighten interest and expectation.
- discuss new or difficult words.
- chat about labels, annotations, and pictures.

Support the reader:

- give the book to the young reader to turn the pages.
- where necessary, encourage longer words to be broken into syllables, sound out each one, and then flow the syllables together; ask him/her to reread the sentence to check the meaning.
- encourage the reader to vary her/his voice as she/he reads; demonstrate how to do this if helpful.

Talk at the end of each book, or after every few pages:

- ask questions about the text and the meaning of the words used—this helps develop comprehension skills.
- read the quiz at the end of the book and encourage the reader to answer the questions, if necessary, by turning back to the relevant pages to find the answers.

Series consultant, Dr. Linda Gambrell, Distinguished Professor of Education at Clemson University, has served as President of the National Reading Conference, the College Reading Association, and the International Reading Association.